A.L. MEADOWS

The Amelia Island Travel Guide

First edition

This book was professionally typeset on Reedsy.
Find out more at reedsy.com

Her soul belongs to summertime; graceful footsteps on warm sands. A heart that leaps in ocean waves; sea salt memory in her hands.

ANGIE WEILAND-CROSBY

Contents

1

WELCOME

Welcome to Amelia Island! This beautiful genteel southern island is located just off the northeastern coast of Florida, and it's a superb spot for a beach vacation. In addition to the pristine beaches for sunbathing and shark tooth hunting, it's home to world-class golfing, shopping, fishing, multiple state parks, delicious restaurants, tons of history to explore and so much more. In this travel guide, I'll give you all the information you need to enjoy Amelia Island to the fullest. I'll tell you about the beaches, my family's favorite restaurants, and what to see and do on the island. However, this guide is by no means an exhaustive resource for everything the island has to offer. My family has been traveling to Amelia Island for over 20 years and there are many things we still have yet to experience. This island immediately grabs you and pulls you into her warm southern hospitality. So whether you're looking for a relaxing getaway or an action-packed adventure, Amelia Island is sure to have something for you. Thanks for choosing my guide, and I hope you have a wonderful time on the island. Don't be surprised if at the end of your vacation you find yourself planning your return to this amazing little island!

The lush canopy drive laden with Spanish Moss you will see on several roads on the island.

2

BRIEF HISTORY OF THE ISLAND

Amelia is a small barrier island located off the coast of Florida in the Atlantic Ocean. The island is named for Princess Amelia, the daughter of King George II of England. Amelia Island has been under the flags of eight different nations throughout its history: France, Spain, Great Britain, the Republic of Florida, the Green Cross of Florida, Mexico, the Confederacy, and the United States.

Amelia's earliest inhabitants were the Timucua Indians, a peaceful and thriving community. The Timucua were masters of the sea, able to navigate the waters around the island with ease. They were excellent farmers, growing crops of maize, beans, and squash. Rich in culture, they were skilled artisans creating beautiful pottery, baskets, and carved wooden masks. The Timucua lived in large communal houses, built from palmetto logs and thatched with palm fronds. They were friendly people, known for their hospitality and generosity, and had their own language, which was distinct from other languages spoken in the area. Sadly, the Timucua were decimated by disease and warfare, and by the early 1800s, they had disappeared from Amelia Island entirely. But their legacy lives on in the names of many of the island's landmarks, including Timucua Point and Timucua Park.

The island also has a long history of piracy dating back to the early 18th century. Pirates such as Blackbeard and Anne Bonny made Amelia Island their base of operations, preying on ships passing through the nearby waters. In 1718, Governor James Moore of South Carolina led an attack on the pirates, destroying their settlements and forcing them to flee.

Despite its turbulent past, Amelia Island is now a popular tourist destination known for its sandy beaches, lush vegetation, and family-friendly destination.

3

GETTING TO THE ISLAND

I f you will be driving your own car to the island, you will enter on one of two bridges.

Southern End: If you are driving up AIA from southern Florida through Atlantic beach, you will need to cross the St. John River via St Johns Ferry located at Mayport Landing. For the schedule and fares please visit (https://ferry.jtafla.com/) before your visit for more information. Once you cross the St. John River you will drive through Fort George Island Cultural State Park, across Fort George River onto Little Talbot Island first, then crossing Simpson Creek you will enter Big Talbot Island. Continuing on A1A you will then cross the George Crady Bridge onto Amelia Island.

Even if you don't enter the park on this end of the island, I highly suggest you take a trip to see this end of the island including Little Talbot and Big Talbot Islands. These are wonderful areas for those who enjoy bird watching and catching a glimpse of the occasional gator and snake! George Crady Bridge Fishing Pier State Park is a wonderful area for fishing or just watching others fish. We have enjoyed catching sharks and tarpon off this pier over the years and the locals are extremely friendly and always ready to share a fish tale!

Western Side: Entering the island on the western side is how the majority of folks drive on the island. Coming from either I95 North or South, you will take Exit 373 to A1A. Following A1A you will cross the Thomas J. Shave Jr. Bridge onto Amelia Island. If you have time to stop and eat, there is a wonderful restaurant located at the bridge called Down Under (https://downunderfb.com). The Down Under has such a wonderful atmosphere and even more delicious food. You will want to start a family tradition of stopping to eat on your way to the island each time you visit!

If you are flying, getting to Amelia by plane is very simple with the use of Jacksonville International Airport (JAX). The airport is serviced by all major airlines with several non-stop trips from major cities. https://www.flyjacksonville.com/

There are many options located on the premises for car rentals at the airport. If you don't have one particular company that you typically use, I'd suggest Googling "rental cars located at Jacksonville International Airport". This will pull up a map to show you those companies at the airport so that you can take a shuttle to the rental lot.

If you're looking for alternatives to renting a car from JAX to Amelia, there are a few other options you can consider. For example, you could take an Uber, Lyft, or private car service. Some options for a private car service include Jacksonville Black Car Limo (https://jacksonvilleblackcarlimo.com/), JAX Black Car (https://jaxblackcar.com/), First Florida Limo (https://firstfloridalimo.com/), and Amelia Airport Shuttle and Transport (https://ameliatransport.com/). If you are staying at either the Omni Amelia Island Plantation Resort or the Ritz Carlton Amelia Island, both provide airport shuttles for their guests. Be sure to speak with the concierge regarding your travel needs when booking your stay.

If you prefer to arrive directly on the island by private jet, you can fly to Fernandina Municipal Airport (https://www.fbfl.us/). From here you can utilize the same private car services to reach your destination, call a Lyft or an Uber or arrange for your resort's shuttle to pick you up.

4

ACCOMMODATIONS

This is by no means an exhaustive list of all the accommodations that Amelia has to offer. These are either the highest-rated accommodations or some of my family's favorites we've visited over the years.

HOTELS AND MOTELS

• **Amelia Hotel At The Beach** (https://ameliahotel.com/)

Looking for a hotel near the beach and close to restaurants. This hotel is located at the intersection of Sadler Road and Fletcher Avenue and is perfect for those who want to enjoy all that the beach has to offer. Just walk across the street and you're there!

You'll also be within walking distance of Dairy Queen, Hammerhead Beach Bar, Slider's Bar and Grill, Seaside Park, the Beach Store, and More, and Amelia Surf Shop. Perfect for families of all sizes, the Amelia Hotel at the Beach offers 89 guest rooms, some with balconies overlooking the beautiful Florida coastline.

- **Beachside Motel** (https://www.beachsidemotel.com/)

Nestled directly on the Amelia Island shoreline, the Beachside Motel is a true hidden gem. With its large pool that overlooks the Atlantic Ocean, complimentary coffee and pastries, and charming two-story design, this small 20-unit motel has been an island staple for many years. And with its convenient location just steps from the beach, it's perfect for a relaxing getaway.

- **Hampton Inn and Suites Amelia Island-Historic Harbor Front** (https://www.hilton.com/)

Looking for a place to stay in Amelia Island that's not on the beach but close to town? Look no further than the Hampton Inn and Suites Amelia Island-Historic Harbor Front. This hotel is located in downtown Fernandina, across from the Oasis Marina, and within walking distance of boutique shops, restaurants, museums, and art galleries. Plus, the harbor is a great spot for watching the sunset! The Hampton Inn and Suites Amelia Island-Historic Harbor Front offer comfortable accommodations and top-notch amenities to make your stay here enjoyable.

- **Residence Inn by Marriott Amelia Island**

(https://Marriott.com)
Looking for a place for an extended vacation or business trip,

Residence Inn by Marriott Amelia Island may be the perfect place for your to stay. Just two blocks from the beach, you can enjoy the sun and surf to your heart's content. If you get tired of sand between your toes, there are plenty of restaurants and shops nearby. And when you're ready to call it a day, the standard rooms or suites will provide everything you need for a comfortable night's sleep.In the morning, start your day with a convenient quick breakfast option. If you're staying in one of the suites, you'll have a kitchenette at your disposal, so you can enjoy a meal in the privacy of your room.

Sunset at the marina.

The on-site gym and pool are also available for your use, as well as an outdoor fire pit for cozy evenings under the stars. Best of all, they're pet-friendly, so you can bring your furry friend along for the ride. They do require a non-refundable pet stay fee and only allow dogs up to 50 pounds.

- **Springhill Suites By Marriott and Courtyard by Marriott**

(https://marriott.com)

SpringHill Suites hotel and Courtyard is conveniently located across the street from Fort Clinch State Park and near Main Beach Park, Fernandina Skate Park, Eagan's Creek Park, Driftwood Surf Shop, and Amelia Lighthouse. Whether you're in town for business or pleasure, this hotel offers everything you need for a comfortable and enjoyable stay. They have spacious suites with plenty of room to spread out, a restaurant on-site for breakfast, a self-service laundry area, a pool, and hot tub, and friendly staff. Two of Amelia's newest hotels, you will find SpringHill Suites and Courtyard to be up-to-date and very clean.

BED AND BREAKFAST AND INNS

- **Addison on Amelia** (https://addisononamelia.com/)

Nestled in the historic downtown of Fernandina, Addison On Amelia is a lovingly maintained bed and breakfast that boasts Southern charm and elegance. Built in 1857 by merchant Frank Simmons, this property features stunning architecture, fifteen gorgeously appointed guest rooms, and a variety of luxurious amenities.

With its 11 ½ foot ceilings, 5 fireplaces, and heart-pine wood floors, the main building at Addison On Amelia is truly breathtaking. Guests will enjoy spending time in the low-country style courtyard, or exploring all that Fernandina has to offer. From its exceptional customer service to its many thoughtful details, Addison On Amelia is sure to become your home away from home.

- **Amelia Island Williams House**

(https://www.williamshouse.com/)
Amelia Island Williams House is a true gem comprising three separate homes with 10 guest rooms. This historic property is located in the village of Fernandina and boasts the distinction of being a Historic Landmark and a must-see for anyone who loves seeing beautiful architecture.

The Williams House, built in 1856, is a beautiful Victorian-style home that was occupied by the Marcus Williams family for over 100 years. The Hearthstone house, built in the 1880s, has Greek Revival influences, and the Carriage house was rebuilt in 2004 in the same location as the original Carriage House.

With wrought iron fences, crystal chandeliers, stained glass, and beautiful antique furniture, guests will be treated to a stay they will never forget. The grand 500-year-old live oak stands proudly in the center of the Great Live Oak Courtyard - truly a sight to behold.

This property is so rich in history and charm, be sure to check out their website before your visit and read about the history of the property and its amazing innkeeper!

- **Amelia Schoolhouse Inn** (https://ameliaschoolhouseinn.com/)

I just love what the owners have done with this historic landmark! The Amelia Schoolhouse Inn on Amelia Island is a one-of-a-kind historic lodging experience. This beautiful inn is located in downtown Fernandina and is just steps away from all the best shopping, dining, and entertainment the island has to offer. The Inn is also centrally located to all of the island's major events, so you'll never miss a beat during your stay.

The Amelia Schoolhouse Inn on Amelia Island offers guests a unique opportunity to step back in time and enjoy all the luxury and comfort of a bygone era. This beautifully appointed inn features all the modern amenities you need for a relaxing stay, while still maintaining the historic charm and character of the original schoolhouse. You'll love spending time in the spacious and well-appointed guest rooms, and you'll appreciate the attentive service of the inn's friendly staff.

If you're looking for an unforgettably romantic getaway or a unique historical vacation experience, look no further than the Amelia School-house Inn on Amelia Island!

Sea turtle tracks

- **Elizabeth Pointe Lodge** (https://elizabethpointeameliaisland.com/)

I truly believe that everyone should stay at one of Elizabeth Pointe Lodge's properties at least once! As soon as you pull in and walk up the stairs to the porch of the lodge, you can feel the southern charm and hospitality oozing out of her walls! If you're looking for a taste of true southern hospitality, look no further than Elizabeth Pointe Lodge. This stunning property offers guests a chance to relax and recharge in one of the most beautiful locations on Amelia Island. Whether you're soaking up the sun on the lodge's private beach or enjoying a refreshing glass of lemonade on the porch, you'll feel right at home at Elizabeth Pointe Lodge.

The guest rooms are beautifully appointed and offer all the amenities you need for a comfortable stay. But it's the little touches that make Elizabeth Pointe Lodge stand out from the crowd. From the rocking chairs on the porch to the chairs and umbrellas at the beach, you'll be treated like royalty from the moment you arrive.

So if you're looking for a truly unique and memorable experience, book your stay at Elizabeth Pointe Lodge today. You won't be disappointed!

- **The Fairbanks House** (https://fairbankshouse.com)

The Fairbanks House is a stunning Italianate villa that offers a romantic escape like no other. With 8,000 square feet of beautifully appointed living space, this home away from home is perfect for couples looking for a luxurious and private getaway. The grounds are impeccably landscaped and feature a variety of romantic amenities, making it the perfect setting for a wedding or intimate getaway. Guests can choose from five rooms in the main mansion, four suites in a separate building, or three cottages adjacent to the property. No matter which accommodation you choose, you'll be treated to stunning views of the lush grounds and surrounded by all the upscale comforts and amenities you could ask for. Located in downtown Fernandina, you're just a short stroll from shops, restaurants, and the marina. Come experience all that the Fairbanks House has to offer!

• **Florida House Inn** (https://floridahouse.com)

Set in the heart of Amelia Island's historic downtown, the Florida House Inn offers guests a taste of true southern charm. This beautiful inn, built in 1857 by railway company founder David Yulee, boasts an array of unique and well-appointed rooms, each with its own history and character.

During the Civil War, the inn was used to house Union Soldiers and later went on to welcome several famous visitors during the Golden Age, including the Vanderbilts and Carnegies. Today, it remains a popular destination for travelers looking to explore all that Amelia Island has to offer. Conveniently located close to boutique shops, restaurants, and the marina, the Florida House Inn is also home to two of the local's favorite spots - The Mermaid Bar and Leddy's Porch. So whether you're looking to relax and enjoy some true southern hospitality or explore all that this island has to offer, the Florida House Inn is sure to make your stay a memorable one.

• **Hoyt House Bed and Breakfast** (https://Hoythouse.com)

The luxurious rooms and top-notch amenities have earned Hoyt House

Bed and Breakfast rave reviews from travelers and critics alike. Built in 1905, the historic inn is styled after the Rockefeller Cottage on Jekyll Island and is the perfect place to escape for a romantic getaway, relaxing weekend, or week-long beach vacation. The 10 beautifully appointed guest rooms are sure to please, and the English pub is the perfect spot to enjoy a pint or two. Plus, their pool and hot tub are the perfect way to unwind after a long day of exploring Amelia Island.

- **Seaside Inn** (https://www.seasideameliainn.com/)

You'll love the central location of this property! Seaside Inn is a 46-room boutique-style hotel located right on Main Beach, so you can enjoy stunning ocean views and easy access to the beach any time you like.

Take a short walk to Fort Clinch State Park, or hop on a bike and head downtown for some shopping and dining. And if you're traveling with young children, they'll love having Main Beach Park right next to the inn – it's perfect for picnics, playground time, and more.

- **Sea Cottages of Amelia** (https://seacottagesofamelia.com/)

Looking for a unique and special place to stay on your next vacation? Look no further than Sea Cottages of Amelia! These beautiful cottages, settled under century-old live oaks, offer guests a true one-of-a-kind experience. Each cottage is equipped with kitchenettes, high-speed internet, and large flat-screen TVs, and is just a block away from the ocean. You'll be within easy walking distance of Dairy Queen, Hammerhead Beach Bar, Slider's Bar and Grill, Seaside Park, the Beach Store, and more when you stay at Sea Cottages of Amelia. And if you need it, some units are even ADA accessible.

RESORTS

- **Omni Amelia Island Resort** - (https://www.omnihotels.com/).

Oh, how my family loves staying at the Omni Amelia Island Resort! Nestled at the southern end of Amelia Island, Omni Amelia Island Resort is a true paradise for those seeking relaxation and luxury. This incredible 1,350-acre community consists of the resort, 900 homes, and 1,200 condominiums, as well as two world-class golf courses, 23 clay tennis courts, delicious restaurants, boutique shops and so much more.

Whether you're looking to enjoy a round of golf on one of the championship courses, take a stroll or bike ride through the stunning live oak and Spanish moss canopy, or simply relax at the luxurious spa, Omni Amelia Island Resort has something for everyone. Do yourself a favor and have breakfast at the Sunrise Cafe and rent a private beach cabana for your stay! (https://AIPCA.net).

- **The Ritz-Carlton** (https://www.ritzcarlton.com/)

This stunning oceanfront resort offers the perfect blend of luxury and relaxation. From the well-known world-class customer service to outstanding amenities, I know you'll enjoy every minute of your stay at the resort.

Located on 1.5 miles of pristine beachfront, there are plenty of ways to enjoy the outdoors. Play tennis or golf on our championship courses, take a dip in one of two pools, or simply relax in a private cabana.

If you're looking for some pampering, the spa is the perfect place to unwind. With a variety of treatments and services available, they always make sure you leave feeling refreshed and rejuvenated.

Whether you want to spend your days exploring Amelia Island or simply relaxing at the resort, I know you'll have an unforgettable experience at the Ritz-Carlton Amelia Island.

HOMES AND CONDOS

If you decide you need more space and privacy for your island vacation, I would suggest one of the gorgeous homes or condos on the island. You will find more options for your stay with one of these choices. However, you must keep in mind that the majority of these have at least a 1-week stay minimum and some will also require a month's long stay.

There are a few ways to find your next rental on Amelia and I highly recommend that if you are planning on staying during a peak time of the year, you book no less than 6 months in advance and 1 year in advance if you can plan that far ahead. Many people return to Amelia year after year and will book their next stay before they leave the island. So, when you find the property you'd like to reserve, jump on it and put a deposit in asap. Below is a list of websites for your reference. There's no need for me to give you a breakdown of each site, as they are self-explanatory. My family and I have stayed in many different accommodations and several different locations on the island. Of course, staying directly on the beach has always been our favorite but over the years we have fallen in love with the entire island and would venture to other parts to experience what those areas had to offer.

- **Amelia Rentals** - https://AmeliaRentals.com
- **Amelia Vacations** - https://AmeliaVacations.com

- **Amelia Island Beachfront Rentals** - https://AmeliaIslandBeachFrontRentals.com
- **VRBO** - https://VRBO.com
- **Amelia Island** - https://AmeilaIsland.com/stay
- **Amelia Island Vacations** - https://AmeliaIslandVacations.com
- **Destination Amelia** - https://DestinationAmelia.com
- **Airbnb** - https://airbnb.com
- **Flip Key from Tripadvisor** - https://flipkey.com
- **Home To Go** - https://HomeToGo.com
- **Vacation Renter** - https://vacationrenter.com
- **Amelia Rentals by Vacasa** - https://www.vacasa.com
- **Moore Amelia Island Rentals** - https://www.mooreairentals.com
- **Amelia Island Premier Beach Rentals** - https://ameliapremierbeachrentals.com/

CAMPING SITES

There are two campsite location options in Fort Clinch State Park. The drive out to both sites through Canopy Drive is gorgeous under Live Oaks and Spanish Moss!

Fort Clinch Amelia River Campground

Located within the boundaries of Fort Clinch State Park, this campground offers 40 campsites, and tent camping is allowed as well. 20-30 amp hookups with water access and a dump station are available here along with laundry facilities for your convenience! If you're looking to enjoy some time by the river while watching out for those dolphins cavorting in their natural habitat then look no further than "Camping near River" - just be sure not to miss sunset when it will seem like they're dancing right before us. https://Campendium.com, https://FlordiaStateParks.org/fortclinch

Fort Clinch State Park -Atlantic Beach Campground

Just like the river campground, this site is also located within the state park on the north end of the island. This campground is small with 20 campsites available and a maximum RV length of 48ft. This site also has hookups, a dump station, laundry facilities, showers, a fire ring, and a picnic area. This is a wonderful location for quiet early morning strolls on the beach as you watch the sunrise and the dolphins swim by. If you love shark tooth hunting as we do, this is another great area to search! https://parkadvisor.com, https://floridastateparks.org

Sunrise at the pier

5

PACKING

There's no doubt about it, Amelia Island is a great place to vacation. But before you pack your bags and head for the Sunshine State, there are a few things you'll need to do to make sure your trip goes off without a hitch.

First, you'll need to decide when you want to visit. Amelia Island is lovely year-round, but the weather can vary depending on the season. Check the weather forecast for the average temperature during the month you will visit so you can pack accordingly. During the summer months, the island is typically hot and humid, so be sure to pack light, airy clothes and sunscreen. In the winter, temperatures are mild but can dip into the 40s at night, so you'll want to bring a jacket or sweater for evenings. If you're looking to spend time outdoors swimming, fishing and other water type activities, late spring through early fall will be the best time to go. However, if you're planning on doing more indoor activities, like visiting museums or shopping, then any time of the year will work. We enjoy the island so much that we've never found a bad time to go. One thing I've learned when traveling to the beach is to always pack a rain jacket and umbrella. Pop-up showers are almost inevitable. I would also suggest packing a light jacket for even the summer months. The wind blowing off the ocean can feel deceptively chilly once the sun goes down.

Next, you'll need to start thinking about what other items you will want to bring. Again, this will depend on the time of year you're traveling. If you're visiting in the summer, you'll obviously need to pack things like swimsuits and lots of sunscreen. Most certainly bring shoes to wear to the beach. Depending on where you are staying, the walk to the beach may be lengthy and the pavement, boardwalks, and sand can be extremely hot to tender feet!

You may need to bring bedding, towels, and toiletries depending on the lodging you have chosen. If you are renting a home for the week, be sure to check with the management company to see if these items are provided. If they are not, ask about paying to have them waiting for you in your rental. This will just eliminate one less thing you need to plan for.

Sunrise after a storm.

You will find that many things can be rented for your use during your time on the island. Later in a subsequent chapter, I will give you the contact information for some of these companies. In our past vacations, we have rented bicycles, beach tents, beach chairs, paddle boards, kayaks, fishing poles, surfboards, and boogie boards.

If you are planning a trip in the winter, Amelia Island can still be quite warm, so you might want to pack to wear layers so you can adjust accordingly. And no matter what time of year you visit, be sure to pack comfortable shoes since you'll likely be doing a lot of walking around!

By following these simple tips, you can ensure that your trip to Amelia Island is everything you've dreamed of - and more!

When you first arrive on the island, you will quickly realize that Amelia is one of Florida's best-kept secrets. Surrounded by pristine beaches and lush marshlands, it's no wonder this island is a popular destination for nature lovers and outdoor enthusiasts. Visitors can expect to find plenty of opportunities for fishing, kayaking, and bird watching. There are also several state parks and conservation areas to explore. And of course, no trip to Amelia Island would be complete without enjoying some of the fresh seafood for which the island is known. Whether you're looking for a relaxing getaway or an adventurous vacation, Amelia Island has something to offer everyone. In the next chapters, I'll cover things to do, things to see, where to get those rentals you may need, and some of the island's amazing restaurants.

6

RENTALS AND SERVICES

When my family and I first started visiting Amelia Island, we would pack EVERYTHING! We looked like the Griswolds or Clampetts rolling into town with the vehicle jam-packed and items strapped to the top and back! Over the years we began to leave things at home, simply because we were tired of dragging them with us. However, we would miss those items. We tried renting our tent and chairs one year and were immediately hooked on the simplicity and convenience. Below is a list of businesses that will help make your trip much simpler and more enjoyable!

The boys tradition of jumping the waves as soon as we arrived at the beach.

- **Amelia Boat Rental** - https://www.ameliaboatrental.com/
- **Amelia Board Rentals** - https://ameliaislandboardrental.com/
- **Amelia Concierges** - http://ameliaconcierges.com/
- **Amelia Island Adventures** - https://ameliaislandadventurerentals.com/
- **Amelia Island Paddle and Surf** - https://www.ameliaislandpaddlesurf.com/
- **Amelia River Cycle** - https://www.ameliarivercycle.com/
- **Amelia Surf Company** - https://ameliasurfco.com/
- **Amelia Wheels** - https://Omnihotels.com - Located on the Plantation, visit the Omni website and search for Amelia Wheels under Activities.
- **Baby Quip** - https://www.babyquip.com/alexa596

27

- **Beach Bikes of Amelia** - https://beachbikesamelia.com/
- **The Beach Store and More** -

https://thebeachstoreandmore.com/

- **Bike Amelia** - https://www.bikeamelia.com/
- **Bike, Scoot, or Yak** - https://www.bikescootoryak.com/
- **Driftwood Surf Shop** - http://driftwoodsurfshop.com/
- **Fernandina Beach Cycling and Fitness** -
- https://www.fernandinabeachcyclingandfitness.com/
- **Kayak Amelia** - https://kayakamelia.com/
- **Pedego Electric Bikes** - https://pedegoelectricbikes.com/
- **PK's Bike Shop** - https://www.pksbikeshop.com/
- **Riptide Water Sports** - https://www.riptidewatersports.com/
- **Road Shark Powersports** - https://roadsharkpowersports.com/
- **Spoke Cycles** - https://spoke-cycles.com/
- **Sunsetter's Beach Rentals** - http://www.sunsettersai.com/
- **Super Corsa Cycles** - https://www.supercorsacycles.com/

7

FISHING AND BOAT TOURS

B oat tours are a great way to see Amelia Island from a different perspective. There are a variety of boat tour companies to choose from, each offering a unique experience. For instance, some boat tours focus on wildlife spotting, while others focus on the history and culture of the island. No matter what you're looking for, there's sure to be a boat tour that's right for you.

Fishing tours are another popular activity on Amelia Island. These tours allow you to relax and enjoy the island's natural beauty while also getting a chance to catch some fish. Whether you're an experienced angler or just getting started, fishing tours are a great way to enjoy the island.

No matter what type of tour you're looking for, Amelia Island has something to offer. With so many options to choose from, you're sure to find the perfect tour for you and your family.

There are so many tours to choose from that I can't do them justice in the confines of this book. However, I'd like to list some for you based on my family's personal experience over the years. We've been on many more and we have never had a bad experience.

- **On The Water Adventures** - http://www.onthewateradventures. com/

On The Water Adventures has been one of my family's all-time favorite boat tours to take year after year. The owner/operator, Captain Carol, knows this island like no other and she is wonderful at tailoring the trip according to what your family would like to see. We have always just let her take us where she thought was the best place to see wildlife that day and she never disappointed us. Captain Carol will do short two-hour trips or all-day trips.We have taken trips up St. Mary's River and we watched the nuclear sub come and go through the canal, we rode over to Cumberland Island and saw so much amazing wildlife including dolphins, manatees, stingrays, and even a shark! Carol has taught us a lot about the history of the island. She is truly a wealth of knowledge. She could even recognize which dolphins were following alongside our boat and had names for each one. I would highly recommend On The Water Adventures to anyone looking for a boat tour in the area.

- **Amelia River Cruises** - http://www.ameliarivercruises.com/

The Amelia River Boat Cruises offers a great way to spend an evening or afternoon with family and friends. You can choose from a variety of cruise options that will suit your needs. The Boat Cruise company also offers special event cruises that are perfect for any occasion. They offer group tours as well as private tours so you can find the perfect fit for your group. The sunset tour is a beautiful way to watch the sun go down over the water. You'll be able to see all the wildlife that comes out at dusk and learn about the history of Amelia Island. The eco-tour is a great way to learn about the ecology of the area and see all the different wildlife up close. No matter which tour you choose, you're sure to have a great time on the Amelia River Boat Cruises.

- **Windward Sailing** - https://windwardsailing.com

You will sigh with relaxation and enjoyment from taking a cruise with Windward Sailing. We've always chosen the catamaran boats but want to do the sailboats sometime shortly. Every time I stepped onto their catamaran boat I would want to cue up the song "Sailing" by Christopher Cross! Windward Sailing offers a wide range of cruise options, from 2-hour excursions to 6-hour adventures. Catamaran boats are available for a more relaxed experience, while sailboats are perfect for those looking for an exhilarating ride. No matter which option you choose, you're sure to enjoy the stunning views of the open water. Our captains have always been very informative about the vessel, the water, and the island. They're also great with kids, and our sailing classes are perfect for those looking to learn more about this fascinating sport. Their sailing classes are on my bucket list of things to do!

- **Amelia Island Charters** - https://ameliaislandcharters.com/

Amelia Island Charters crew is a very professional and experienced staff and will make sure you have a great time out on the water, whether you're a seasoned fisherman or just trying it for the first time.

They offer a variety of charter fishing packages to suit any budget and group size and also provide all the equipment you'll need, including rods, reels, and bait. All you need to bring is yourself, some sunscreen, and a sense of adventure!

- **Fish Amelia Island** - https://fishameliaisland.com

When you book a fishing adventure with Captain Danny, you're in for a treat. Not only is he an expert fisherman, but he's also a great guide. He'll take you to all the best spots on Fish Amelia Island, and we have always caught fish each time we went out.

Captain Danny is fun to be around, and he knows all the best spots on the island. You'll have a great time whether you're catching fish or just enjoying the scenery. And when you do catch fish, you'll be sure to enjoy them. Captain Danny will clean and filet your fish for you, so you can just sit back and relax.

- **Amelia Fishing Adventures** - https://www.ameliafishingadventures.com/

If you're looking for an incredible fishing adventure, look no further than Amelia Fishing Adventures. Captain Jeremiah is an expert in both saltwater and freshwater fishing and knows all the best spots in the area. No matter what kind of fish you're hoping to catch, he'll make sure you have a great time and come home with a big haul.

His boats are top-of-the-line and their equipment is top-notch.They take care of everything so you can relax and enjoy your time on the water.

- **Big Fin Fishing Charters** - http://www.bigfincharters.com/

We had an excellent fishing experience as a family with Big Fin Fishing. Our captain was wonderful with our boys, keeping them engaged the entire trip. We had a fun day moving around the water and catching several different types of fish. They make everything simple for you by having all the tackle and bait ready to go. You just show up with sunscreen and cameras to capture the picture of your big catch!

Shrimp Boats

8

FESTIVALS AND EVENTS

Amelia Island is home to many events and festivals throughout the year, from music festivals to art shows. The island hosts several major events, such as the Amelia Island Concours d'Elegance and the Isle of Eight Flags Shrimp Festival. Many smaller events take place throughout the year, including concerts and food festivals. If you're looking for something fun to do, be sure to check out the upcoming events on Amelia Island You're sure to find something that interests you! Be sure to check out the ever-changing calendar at https://ameliaisland.com/calendar. Below are a few of the major events that might interest you.

- **Amelia Island Jazz Festival**

https://ameliaislandjazzfestival.com/
Amelia Island is home to many different and exciting annual events, including the Amelia Island Jazz Festival. Scheduled on different dates each year and lasting one full week, this event features some of the biggest names in jazz. If you're looking for a fun and unique way

to spend your vacation, be sure to check out this incredible event! The festival will take place at venues all over Amelia Island, so there's something for everyone. Whether you're a jazz lover or just looking for a good time, the Amelia Island Jazz Festival is not to be missed.

- **Dickens on Centre** - http://ameliaislandtdc.com/

December on Amelia Island is a truly magical time. For one special weekend, the island comes alive with a Victorian-themed Christmas celebration - Dickens On Centre. Downtown streets are lined with musicians, carolers, vendors, and artists, and the whole island is aglow with Christmas lights and decorations. Visitors can watch a production of The Christmas Carol on the Main Stage, visit the Enchanted Village, or stick around for Dickens After Dark, an adults-only event. No matter what you choose to do, you're sure to enjoy the festive atmosphere and experience the joy of Christmas on Amelia Island.

- **Isle of Eight Flags Shrimp Festival**

https://www.shrimpfestival.com/

If you only attend one event on the island, this is it! This festival is a food lover's paradise, with shrimp being the star of the show. But there's also plenty of other seafood on offer, as well as a range of other dishes for those who don't love seafood. And of course, there's also a selection of drinks to enjoy.

But the Shrimp Festival is about more than just food. There's also plenty of entertainment to enjoy, with live music on offer throughout the festival. There are also arts and crafts stalls, and a parade which is always a highlight.

And if you're feeling competitive, you can take part in the Shrimp Run, the Festival Pageant, the Arts and Craft Shows, and various other events.

So whether you're a foodie, an entertainer, or just looking for a fun day out, the Shrimp Festival is the perfect event for you. Visit the website to find out more and plan your trip.

- **Amelia Island Courcours d'Elegance** - https://carcollectorsclub. com/, https://ameliaIsland.com/calendar

The Amelia Island Concours d'Elegance is a three-day celebration of all things automotive. The event includes car themed-events, entertainment, luxury shopping, auctions, seminars, new vehicle driving experiences, and a Cars & Coffee Saturday. The celebration concludes on Sunday with the Concours d'Elegance, a showcase of the world's most beautiful and rare cars.

The Amelia Island Concours d'Elegance is hosted by the Amelia Island Foundation, a non-profit organization dedicated to preserving and promoting the history and heritage of Amelia Island. Proceeds from the event benefit the foundation and its programs.

9

THINGS TO DO ON THE ISLAND

The things you can do on this island seem endless! It all depends on what you are interested in and how much activity you like to do. Below is a list of ideas but by no means exhaustive! Of course, spending the day at the beach! Fernandina is a wonderful beach to play on with kids whether you are building sand castles, riding bikes, playing ball, throwing a frisbee, looking for shark teeth, or fishing from the beach. The beach is nice and broad and allows ample space to spread out and play.

1. **Fishing** - There are many places and ways to fish on Amelia Island. You can fish from the piers, bridges, rivers, surf fishing, inlet fishing, or deep sea fishing. Be sure to check out the guided tours I have listed as well.
2. **Bike Riding** - Amelia Island is a biker's paradise. The beaches are an easy area to ride when the tide is low. The beaches are broad and packed nicely which makes for an easy ride. Fort Clinch State Park is a great choice along with Eagan's Creek Greenway, Amelia Island Trail, River Island Trail, and just around the island

in general.

3. **Boat Tours** - There are many different boat tours and boat companies around the island that will give many different types of guided tours. Be sure to check out some of the ones I've listed.

4. **Cumberland Island** - take a day trip and visit Cumberland Island. They have an amazing hiking trail, beautiful beaches, and wild horses to see. You can walk out to see the ruins of the Dungeness Mansion or visit Plum Orchard Mansion.

5. **Spa Day** - Several wonderful spas around the island are ready to pamper and relax you.

6. **Visit Amelia Lighthouse**

7. **Play Putt-Putt** - Amelia has three different locations for Putt Putt. Putt Putt Fun Center, Island Falls Adventure, and Heron's Cove Adventure Golf.

8. **Shopping** - Amelia has many wonderful boutique shops to meander through and find that special gift to take home from your vacation.

9. **Visit the Amelia Island Museum Of History**

10. **Visit an art gallery on the island**

11. **Rent a paddle board, surfboard, kayak, hydro bike, or moped and explore!**

12. **Go hiking!** Amelia has some wonderful hiking trails to explore. There's Egan's Creek Greenway, Fort Clinch State Park, Amelia Island Trail, Little Talbot Island, Big Talbot Island, and then over to Cumberland Island. A small word of warning for those of you who are not used to hiking in the south. First, take and wear bug spray. Second, take water. Third, watch for wildlife! Amelia has some dangerous wildlife that needs to be respected to prevent any harm that may come to you or the wildlife. The island does have venomous snakes as well as alligators. Incidents are very rare but just be mindful of where you are walking and sitting. 85% of snake

bites occur when someone tries to capture or kill a snake. Just leave them alone and they'll leave you alone.

13. **Ride horses on the beach!** Check out these companies for an amazing experience - Amelia Island Horseback Riding -https://ameliaislandhorsebackriding.com/, Happy Trails Walking Horses - https://www.happytrailswalkers.com/, and Kelly's Seahorse Ranch - http://www.kellyranchinc.net/

14. **Play golf at one of the beautiful courses on the island.** Omni Amelia Island Resort - Oak Marsh, Amelia River Golf Club, Fernandina Beach Golf Club, The Golf Club of Amelia Island, The Golf Club at North Hampton, Amelia National Golf and Country Club, The Amelia Island Club at Long Point.

15. **Look for sea turtle nests.** Depending on the time of year you travel to the island, you may be one of the fortunate ones to be able to see the large sea turtle tracks or the little ones making their way to the surf after they hatch. Please be respectful of the nests and the turtles and leave them alone. If you would like to educate yourself about these amazing creatures and how to protect them, I would suggest looking into this website. https://ameliaislandseaturtlewatch.com/

10

RESTAURANTS

Food is an important part of your vacation and if you're a foodie, Amelia Island is sure to delight you! There are so many wonderful restaurants that it's simply impossible to list them all. They need a guide all of their own! I will list some of my family's favorites for you.

- **Salty Pelican Bar and Grill** - https://thesaltypelicanamelia.com/

The Salty Pelican has a great beach atmosphere down near the marina. It's a great place to stop in to eat after an afternoon of shopping or take a stroll along the marina after you've stuffed yourself with a meal!

- **4th Street Deli** - https://www.4thstreetdeli.com/

When my family is asked where they want to get lunch or take out while we are on Amelia, 9 times out of 10, they will say 4th Street Deli. Everything is so fresh and delicious and the salad selection is amazing. The owners are so friendly and kind!

- **Down Under Restaurant** - http://www.downunderfb.com/

Located at the bridge as you enter the western side of the island, Down Under has been a delight on the island for years. Great atmosphere and delicious food!

- **Tasty's Fresh Burgers** - https://tastysfreshburgersandfries.com/

This is a small chain restaurant that is located in a renovated gas station downtown. My kids love to get a burger with shugga butta sweet potato fries. Yes, they are as good as they sound!

- **Sunrise Cafe** - Located at the Omni Amelia Island Plantation. If you're staying on the Plantation, you don't want to miss this one! This is a scrumptious breakfast buffet with Belgian waffles, fresh fruits, cheeses, omelets, sausage, bacon, and pastries. Grab your plate of deliciousness and go sit on the deck overlooking the Atlantic Ocean. Sunday Brunch is my favorite as there is usually a live band playing!

- **The Happy Tomato Courtyard Cafe and BBQ** - https://www.th ehappytomatocafe.com/

We simply love this little restaurant for its outdoor seating. They have a simple yet delicious menu of BBQ and assorted sandwiches and salads along with chocolate chip cookies all tucked in a side street under a canopy of umbrellas.

- **Timoti's Seafood Shak** - http://www.timotis.com/

If seafood is what you want but you're looking for something a little more unique, you can't go wrong with Timoti's. They have everything from Tacos to Poke Bowls.

- **Cafe Karibo** - https://www.cafekaribo.com/

A favorite to many. This eclectic restaurant has a little something for everyone. Yum!

- **Sliders Seaside Grill** - https://www.slidersseaside.com/

Sliders have been an island staple since 1945 starting out as a roadhouse. In 2003 it was completely renovated and now is a popular bar and grill directly on the beach with live music.

- **Bob's Steak and Chop House** - https://bobs-steakandchop.com/amelia-island

Really good steaks and seafood to be a chain restaurant with a great atmosphere.

- **David's Restaurant and Lounge** - https://www.ameliaislanddavids.com/

Gorgeous restaurant with an eclectic menu to satisfy even the most discerning taste buds. This is not a restaurant for small children unless they have a fairly advanced palate but the adults will most certainly enjoy it.

The island also has several grocery stores conveniently located around the island. And now that most have pick-up or delivery, we find it very easy to place an order on the way to the island and pick it up on our way into our accommodation or have it delivered.

Also, another other business I'd like to recommend to you is **Amelia To Go** (https://www.ameliatogo.com/). Simply go to their website and choose from one of their participating restaurants. They will deliver to your hotel, marina, park or even the beach! You can sit on the beach with your toes in the sand and enjoy the warm ocean breezes and wait for your food to be hand delivered to you. I'm all about convenience, especially when I'm on vacation!

11

CONCLUSION

Amelia Island has been a special place for my family for many years. We love that we can go back year after year to the same locations, restaurants and take the same tours and it feel like we're at home. We have jars of shells, shark teeth, sand dollars and sea glass sitting around our home. They are beautiful but also reminders of the wonderful times Amelia Island has shared with us. Time is very short, so make memories with those you love!

I am thankful that you chose to purchase The Amelia Island Travel Guide. My family has fallen in love with this beautiful island over the years, and we sincerely hope you and your family get to experience its magic firsthand. **If you enjoyed the book, please leave a positive review on Amazon! It would mean a great deal to me and future readers.**

Seashells, sea glass, & shark teeth our family has collected on Amelia.

12

RESOURCES

History of Amelia. (n.d.). Https://www.Exploreamelia.com/. Retrieved 1 September 2022, from https://www.exploreamelia.com/Amelia_Island_History.shtml

Jacksonville Transportation Authority. (n.d.). *Information.* https://Ferry.Jtafla.com. Retrieved 1 September 2022, from https://ferry.jtafla.com/#info

Down Under. (2022). *Welcome To Our Place.* http://www.Downunderfb.com/. Retrieved 1 September 2022, from http://www.downunderfb.com/

Amelia Hotel At The Beach. (n.d.). *The Hotel.* https://Ameliahotel.Com/Amelia-Island- Hotel/. Retrieved 1 September 2022, from https://ameliahotel.com/amelia-island-hotel/

Beachside Motel. (n.d.). *Beachside Motel.* Https://www.Beachside

motel.com/. Retrieved 31 August 2022, from https://www.beachsid
e
motel.com/

Hilton. (2022). *Hotel Info.* https://www.Hilton.com. Retrieved 31
August 2022, from
Marriott. (2022). *Residence Inn by Marriott Amelia Island Find Hotel.*
https://Www.Marriott.com. Retrieved 1 September 2022, from
https://www.marriott.com/search/findHotels.mi

Addison On Amelia. (2022). *Discover Our Amelia Island Inn.* https://A
ddisononamelia.
com. Retrieved 1 September 2022, from https://addisononamelia.c
om/inn/

Amelia Island Williams House. (2022). *History Of The Inn.* Https://www.
Williamshouse.com. Retrieved 31 August 2022, from https://www.
williamshouse.com/history

Addison On Amelia. (2022). *Discover Our Amelia Island Inn.* https://A
ddisononamelia.
com. Retrieved 1 September 2022, from https://addisononamelia.c
om/inn/

Elizabeth Pointe. (2021). *Accomodations.* https://Elizabethpointeameli
aisland.com.
Retrieved 30 August 2022, from https://elizabethpointeameliaislan
d.com/accomodations

Fairbanks House. (2022). *About The Inn.* Https://Fairbankshouse.com.
Retrieved 30

RESOURCES

August 2022, from https://fairbankshouse.com/the-inn/

Saltmarsh Hospitality Group LLC Company. (2022). *History.* https://www.
    Floridahouse.com. Retrieved 27 August 2022, from https://www.fl oridahouse.com/history

Hoyt House. (2022). *About The Hoyt House Inn.* https://Hoythouse.com. Retrieved 1
    September 2022, from https://hoythouse.com/about-the-inn/

Bee Loud Digital Marketing. (2022). *Property.* https://www.Seaside ameliainn.com.
    Retrieved 1 September 2022, from https://www.seasideameliainn.c om/property/

Sea Cottages Of Amelia. (2022). *About.* https://www.Seacottagesofam elia.com.
    Retrieved 31 August 2022, from https://www.seacottagesofamelia.c om

Omni Hotels & Resorts. (2022). *About.* https://www.Omnihotels.com /Hotels/Amelia-
    Island. Retrieved 1 September 2022, from
    The Ritz-Carlton Hotel Company, L.L.C. (2022). *Hotel Overview.* https://www.Ritzcarlton.com/En/Hotels/Florida/Amelia-Island. Retrieved 31 August
    2022, from https://www.ritzcarlton.com/en/hotels/florida/amelia-island/hotel-overview

Campendium Inc. (2022). *Amelia River Campground.* https://Campen

49

dium.com.
Retrieved 1 September 2022, from https://www.campendium.com/
amelia-river-
campground-fort-clinch-sp

Florida Department of Environmental Protection. (2022). *Fort Clinch State Park.* https://www.Floridastateparks.org/. Retrieved 30 August 2022, from https://www.floridastateparks.org/index.php/fortclinch

ParkAdvisor LLC. (2022). *Fort Clinch State Park - Atlantic Beach Campground.* https://Parkadvisor.com. Retrieved 1 September 2022, from https://www.parkadvisor.com/us/florida/fernandina+beach/51922/Fort+Clinch+State+
Park+Atlantic+Beach+Campground

CAPT. CAROL. (2019). *About.* Http://Www.Onthewateradventures.Com. Retrieved 1
September 2022, from http://www.onthewateradventures.com

Amelia River Cruises. (n.d.). *Cruises.* https://Ameliarivercruises.com/. Retrieved 1
September 2022, from https://ameliarivercruises.com/cruises/

Windward Sailing. (n.d.). *Home.* https://Windwardsailing.com/. Retrieved 2 September
2022, from https://windwardsailing.com/

Amelia Island Charters. (2022). *Fishing Charters.* https://Ameliaisland
charters.com/.
Retrieved 2 September 2022, from Fish Amelia Island. (n.d.). *Home.*
http://www.Fishameliaisland.com/. Retrieved 2 September 2022,

from
http://www.fishameliaisland.com/

Amelia Fishing Adventures. (2019). *About*. https://www.Ameliafishin
gadventures.
com/. Retrieved 2 September 2022, from

BIGFIN CHARTERS. (2018). *About*. Http://www.Bigfincharters.com/.
Retrieved 2
September 2022, from http://www.bigfincharters.com/

Amelia Island Tourist Development Council. (n.d.). *Calendar*.
https://Ameliaisland.com.
Retrieved 2 September 2022, from https://ameliaisland.com/calend
ar

Amelia Island Jazz Festival, Inc. (2022). *About The Festival*. https://Am
eliaislandjazz
festival.com. Retrieved 2 September 2022, from https://ameliaislan
djazzfestival.com/
about-the-amelia-island-jazz-festival/

Amelia Island Tourist Development Council. (n.d.-b). *Events*.
http://Ameliaislandtdc.com
/Events. Retrieved 2 September 2022, from http://ameliaislandtdc.
com/events

Isle of Eight Flags Shrimp Festival in Fernandina Beach, FL. (2022).
History. Https://Www.Shrimpfestival.Com. Retrieved 2 September
2022, from https://www.shrimpfestival.com/history/

CarCollectorsClub.com. (2022). *Amelia Island Concours d'Elegance.* Https://Carcollectorsclub.Com. Retrieved 2 September 2022, from https://carcollectorsclub.com/event/the-amelia-island-concours-d elegance-car-show-
event-march-3-6-2022/

Salty Pelican. (n.d.). *About.* https://Thesaltypelicanamelia.com. Retrieved 2 September
2022, from https://thesaltypelicanamelia.com/about-us/

4th Street Deli & Salads. (2022). *4th Street Deli.* Retrieved 2 September 2022,
from https://www.4thstreetdeli.com/

Tasty's Fresh Burgers. (n.d.). *Locations.* Https://Tastysfreshburgersan dfries.Com/.
Retrieved 2 September 2022, from https://tastysfreshburgersandfri es.com/
locations/

The Happy Tomato Courtyard Cafe & BBQ. (n.d.). *Home.* https://Www.Thehappytomatocafe.Com/. Retrieved 2 September
2022, from https://www.thehappytomatocafe.com/

Timbotis. (n.d.). *Home.* Http://Www.Timotis.Com/. Retrieved 2 September 2022, from http://www.timotis.com/

Cafe Karibo. (n.d.). *Home.* Https://Www.Cafekaribo.Com. Retrieved 2 September
2022, from https://www.cafekaribo.com

RESOURCES

Sliders Sea Side. (n.d.). *Our History.* Https://Www.Slidersseaside.Com/. Retrieved
  2 September 2022, from https://www.slidersseaside.com/our-histo
ry

Bob's Steak & Chop House. (2022). *Bob's Steak & Chop House - Amelia Island.* Https://
  Bobs-Steakandchop.Com.   Retrieved 2 September 2022, from https://bobs-
  steakandchop.com/amelia-island/

David's.   (2022).   *About.*   Https://Www.Ameliaislanddavids.Com. Retrieved 2 September
  2022, from https://www.ameliaislanddavids.com/about

Amelia To Go, LLC. (2022). *Home.* Https://Www.Ameliatogo.Com. Retrieved 2
  September 2022, from https://www.ameliatogo.com

Weiland-Crosby, A. (2020). *Beach Quotes.* Https://Www.Momsoulsoothers.
  com/Summer-Quotes-with-a-Splash-of-Soul/. Retrieved 2 September

  2022, from https://www.momsoulsoothers.com/summer-quotes-with-
  a-splash-of-soul/

Printed in Great Britain
by Amazon

26179462R00036